The
Other
Side
of
Beauty

Also by Garrett Rittenberg

South American Scenes
Italian Sketches

The Other Side of Beauty

Garrett Rittenberg

Bowery Books
New York

ISBN: 978-1-7344202-7-2

For André Leon Talley

"If you don't know where you are, you probably don't know who you are."

—Ralph Ellison, *Invisible Man*

Contents

The Other Side of Beauty

Dear André,

I appreciate your long and inquisitive note about my most recent travels. It is not often I receive so many questions all at once and with interest so considerable. I had a feeling you might be interested in my recent travels, but it was still a pleasant surprise to receive your message. It feels as though they took place years rather than months ago, because of all that has happened since. Nonetheless, the time that has passed has given me a chance to reflect on where I have been and what I have seen.

I have been painting vociferously since I returned and with much success. When I say success I speak in terms of how able I am in expressing myself, which is my main concern when faced with a blank canvas. I am always looking for beauty, something to please my eye and that of others. I am always in search of a beautiful scene. When it comes to writing, there is a similar search taking place. Some are gifted enough to make beautiful words seamlessly pour out of a pen, but so often the most well written and meaningful collections of words take time and contemplation. Such things require work, but there is also the need for moments of revelation. Those revelatory moments can be brought on by the multitude of experiences that abound or they are simply given to us through the words of another person.

Your powers of intuition are rubbing off on me. Little by little I get a better sense of things on the horizon. Just before I read your note, I thought of something you had once said to me. I am not sure if you remember this, but it was during a time when I was experiencing a sort of creative void, more specifically, I had been unsuccessful in my search for a new subject to paint. It felt like a kind of writer's block, a lull in creative output. Such feelings can leave an artist thinking they will never create or work again. I was rather prolific up to that point, and upon mentioning this you offered some terse, yet sufficient advice. I remember your words like this, "keep painting, keep going, keep searching for the other side of beauty." I was struck by the boldness and brevity of such a phrase. I quickly wrote it down, in fact I wrote it down a few times over the following days. It made me happy each time I wrote it down and it continued to remain fresh in my mind. I regularly thought of the phrase, at times baffled, while at other times completely motivated and creatively inspired by it. Beauty is beauty, I thought. There is no other side or is everything beautiful in its own way? I thought lazily about the clichéd phrase of beauty being in the eye of the beholder. I was dissatisfied by each of the explanations that came to mind, but I enjoyed the mystery of your phrase more than anything, not knowing where to apply it nor completely understanding it. It gave 'the other side' an air of endless possibility. It was a phrase that enabled me to constantly look at things differently in both art and life. Nonetheless I have kept it with me. I never wanted you to expand on what you meant, nor did I want you to clarify it. It was enough of a gift. When you said it, the words alone had enough of a clarifying effect and I was no longer in doubt about my ability to find something worth painting, which came to fruition shortly thereafter.

After considering all the questions you have put before me, I thought it only fitting to reply to your note in great detail. No one else asks me the kinds of questions you do, and to be faced with so many that are indeed good and precise, is a flattering occurrence. You are curious to know much, just as I am. It has taken me some time to think about each question, because they inevitably lead to more than one answer or involve considerable description. I say this gratefully, not only for their thoughtfulness, but because they require and inspire me to think deeply about what I have experienced.

This letter may appear long, but I hope it is only because of the infrequency of receiving letters of such length. When I think about the length of this letter, when I think of you, I realize there are so many things we do not say to each other. As much as we do say and write to one another, there is still so much left unsaid. Silence, so often, is the way of man. Even the garrulous can be shy, tongue-tied, afraid, and lack the strength to tell the truth or the will to express themselves. Your questions have given me strength, your curiosity has fueled my expression, and your interest has encouraged me to no longer be silent. In a way, your questions and your interest, raise me up and I feel as though I am on a stage when I speak to you. You are one person, but your opinions are as powerful as the cheers or boos of an esteemed audience.

As you know, my travels have been an education for me, steadily guiding me through each of life's destinations thus far. I have spoken to you at length about much of my travels, but I have not spoken to you in any great detail about India; what I have experienced there and what it has done for me. With this most recent visit I am even more inclined to share some of my thoughts and stories with you. I am happy for the opportunity to reveal these thoughts, and I would not have been as inclined had it not been for your curiosity.

As I write this letter, I ask myself, who am I to speak on a place as ancient and historically rich as India? I am not a scholar of that country or its culture, and would not dare to consider myself anything other than an admirer and observer of it. But I feel inclined out of a love and fascination for that land, even more so since you desire to know what I think. It is best to say that I am familiar with India, and I know quite a bit about it as a matter of fact, at least enough to articulate what I have experienced. In a sense it is a delightful position to find myself in, yet in another it leaves me with a void, for as much as I have experienced I still feel as if I have merely walked into the first room of a large castle. India is indeed a great castle of a subject, a glittering palace, a Versailles, a Chatsworth, a place that takes years to see all the details and understand completely. At times it is impenetrable and can swat away even the nicest and most genuine of admirers. The fine details appear complex, because of my own ignorance and the uncertainty of experiencing something different, something unknown, something new.

I have always wanted to say something about India ever since my first visit when I was twenty-one-years-old. But what could I say about a country such as India after one visit and reading a dozen or so books? Furthermore, what could I say after reading the works of V.S. Naipaul? For it seems futile to try and say it more concisely than him. I have never lived there, I am not an Indian myself, if anything it would take much more studying and several more extended visits. Besides, India like so many other things in life, should not necessarily be understood completely. Any attempt to do so by a westerner or for that matter, any other foreigner would take much too long to fully comprehend its complexity. For the novice, it is good enough to have experienced India, that in itself will always be something. After all, experiences are a beginning.

When you ask why I go to such places, I am unsure

how to respond at first, but I tend to surmise that it can be swiftly narrowed down to wanderlust. That well of energy that is characteristic of an impatient and restless being. Wanderlust can be born out of a dissatisfaction with sitting in one place for too long, coupled with a distaste for the sedentary life. Stillness can have a delineating effect upon the mind, even if one is indeed, busy. A man's wanderlust can be a rejection of the domestic and the static, it could also simply be the conscious decision that it is just time to go. We are a nomadic species and it seems mostly a matter of fate that I possess an excess amount of this most human characteristic.

It is natural and human to be moving; for centuries, life for generations of people has involved moving, migrating, fleeing, seeking, and quite simply just going for the sake of it. And so for me it feels natural to be going some place else, just like so many of my fellow human beings have done for one reason or another. It is only strange or impressive to those who do not wish to do the same. To be in one place for too long plagues me with the dreadful feeling that comes when my time is being wasted. To be busy, in and of itself, is a kind of life for many and can often blind one from the many beautiful things that exist on this earth. It can indeed blind one from that most precious possession called time. Being busy is good, but so often that involves the drudgeries of domestic and office life. I prefer to be busy going somewhere.

I went to India a second time out of a great desire to

return to a place I had once been, because my previous visit was a profound and life altering journey. It was an experience that changed my mind and continually shaped it long after the journey had finished. There were many things I was confronted by in that first trip that were difficult to understand and equally difficult to accept. The cultural differences were many, but nonetheless were a disruptive and blunt method for learning about a place and about oneself. When you are in India, you are undoubtably in it; it is impossible to mistake where one might be, and hard to not be influenced by it in some way. India gets right up next to you and does not leave you alone until you are out of its airspace. However, even after I had left, so much of it had remained with me.

My two journeys were separated by twelve-years and they were years filled with both nostalgia for what I had experienced and a yearning to return. During that month-long journey I was accompanied by two pretty English girls, my then girlfriend and her sister. We circled around the country for a month, mostly by train, starting and ending in Mumbai, staying in most every interesting place along the way for a couple of days, from Jaipur to Agra to Varanasi to Kolkata to Hampi and the beaches of Goa. The first visit was such a formative experience that I began to use that month-long trip as a lens through which to understand a great deal of what life would put before me thereafter. It was an experience I always thought about because it profoundly altered my perspective, my sense of reality, and challenged every concept of normalcy I previously held. It was an assault on all the senses. The difficulties of travel were magnified not only because I was twenty-one-years-old, but because it was the month of May, which meant one-hundred-and-ten degree temperatures across the country. It was a trip that I was nostalgic for before it even ended, and with time the trip only became more influential. It was merely one month of my life, but it was worth years in terms of experience and education.

After thinking about India for twelve-years I naturally wanted to say something meaningful about it. My youth and naivety were indeed significant factors to my initial experiences, and to speak on India properly I understood I would need distance from it and to make a return journey in order to better grasp where I had been. By revisiting, much like rereading, I would be better able to understand my first journey and the country itself in both the past and the present.

India is a world unto itself and difficult to navigate. All the cultural and customary differences force one to make mental adjustments that most are simply not willing or even capable of making. The blunt realities of life on display on the sub-continent can greatly affect the psyche of any young person, especially that of a westerner.

The simplest of scenes remain vivid to me. One of the first was while walking through a slum in Mumbai. The heat was oppressive and suffocating like having a plastic bag over my head, and I walked through the streets quickly taking in the intense scenes of impoverishment. I went down one particular street and life seemed to steadily get worse for all the people who populated it the further along I went. The heat only added to the misery. The disabled and beleaguered were stuck in one spot left to beg for whatever pittances passersby were willing to give. Their clothes were tattered and dirty and their hair looked sadly similar to their clothing. Older men were terribly skinny and their hair which had gone white was made artificially dark through days, weeks or months of accumulating dust and dirt. In the few moments I witnessed these men, it indeed seemed like an eternity. It was obvious that they had been there for a long time, and it was equally obvious that they were not going to escape that situation. Along with the sight of crippled homeless men was the equally difficult reality of seeing little children begging on the street. One boy, who I assume was four or five-years-old approached me to ask for some money, all the while carrying his two-year-old brother on his back, neither of them wearing a single piece of clothing.

Within feet of each other were crippled men in a haggard state and unclothed boys asking strangers for money. I was saddened, for it seemed to be the beginning and end of what life is like in India all in one scene; fate just a few feet away from hope. I gave the boys and a few of the men some Rupees, and it felt like throwing pennies into an ocean with unreasonable wishes. I knew it would fix nothing. There was nothing in that moment I could do to fix anything. These struggles, these circumstances were a part of something that could not be solved merely through charitable acts. Never in my life had I been in the presence of human beings whose lives, whose chances were so completely and utterly wrecked.

There were several cows in the street and all I knew was that they were considered holy to Hindus, and of course never to be eaten. But they were not well fed nor taken good care of, they were merely left alone. It was peculiar to see an animal considered sacred, not grazing upon some lush meadow, but rather sat in the middle of a desolate street in danger of being run over or in to by some passing vehicle or motorbike. They were somehow never touched as the chaotic scene was not entirely chaotic. It was chaotic to me, but it was normal for those who lived there. The motorbikes, Tuk-Tuks, pushcarts and taxis wove through the street somehow missing the people and cows that populated it. It was a anarchic scene to me and difficult to take in, but it was merely another day for everyone who called this street home. I was struck by that fact and had to regularly remind myself that this was indeed the home of many people. I was made constantly aware that I was not home, and that my home was profoundly different.

I soon witnessed a fight in the middle of a street between two middle-aged-men with lithe bodies throwing vicious windmill punches that rarely connected. I had not a clue what they were fighting about, but each of their faces carried the most intense and decisive expressions of wanting to kill the man in front of him. The traffic of the street swerved around the changing positions of the two men just as it had swerved around the sacred cows. For a moment I delighted in the similarity of something holy and something dangerous being avoided in the same manner. The fight ended after about twenty or so punches thrown by each man, followed by the shouting of insults before the two were separated by their disgust with the sight of one another. No one tried to intervene and the traffic never ceased. Only those that had been part of the events leading up to the fight gave any attention to the fracas. The two men showed no signs of exhaustion or fear. They were content and went back to work.

Each scene in the streets I observed was made more worrisome by the backdrop of derelict buildings and primitive shacks that lined many of the streets. Their collapse looked imminent. Electric wires decorated each structure like ivy gone mad, but there was no beauty in this sort of overgrowth as there is in an overgrown jungle. This was merely modernity in a state of disastrous failure. There were streets that were open air hardware stores with small shack-like structures, each selling a different piece of equipment; nuts, bolts, bags of concrete, and all manner of metal materials and building supplies. It all added to the incomplete feel of the neighborhood. The whole place was like a building site that was never finished, yet it was where so many people lived and worked.

When looking at such scenes I could not help, but think that life is a never ending procession of random instances of misery. I could make attempts to explain as to why those conditions existed and why they are likely to remain, but ultimately they are predictions, musings, and intellectual fodder. It is a subject for the historians, sociologists and economists and there is no need to harp on the history of a circumstance. History is not always helpful. Some things will change, others will go on. All that matters is what is done next.

I started to consider the possibility that life is just a great tragedy. More often than not, religions teach that there is righteousness in poverty, that there is holiness in suffering. It is hard for me to agree with such sentiments after seeing people living on the street and in pain, with stress and without a way out. I dismissed this belief, because when suffering looks you in your eyes you must conclude that there is nothing righteous about it and that righteousness does not give meaning to anything that exists in reality. Difficult circumstances are an unfortunate loss of time. To call a man righteous for suffering strips him of his dignity and dismisses his pain; distracting him from the realization that pain is something we experience alone.

It all felt like a visual assault that one had to just deal with and accept in order to get down the street, get through the day and to get home. Everything was new and somewhat shocking to my young mind, but could ultimately be dealt with by looking away or just dealing with things as they happened. What was more of a constant difficulty was the oppressive heat and the powerful sun. The heat magnified the difficulty of everything going on. While I was considering the harsh circumstances of life on the street, I was forced to factor in the crushing nature of an unforgiving climate. If these people were living in a constant fight it was as if they were being hit from every angle. They appeared trapped, boxed in, and sadly at times I found myself thinking of those streets and their homes as a kind of prison.

It is always jarring to hear someone ask me about my clothes, and were anyone other than you to ask me such questions I would brush it aside and probably even laugh it off without paying it too much mind, but since you are an authority of such things, I fall in line and confess my faults in wearing colors that do not particularly compliment this Indian setting. You intuitively knew the excuse for my heedless choices. I admit, indeed, the heat does take away the brain power and head space once reserved for thoughtful clothing choices. I suppose the consequences of such decisions result in one wearing far too much grey or navy blue. Though, at times I have been wearing more colorful clothing, I must confess that the climate is not the sole factor for my tendency of dressing down.

Truthfully, every time I wore a bright-color-shirt or pants I was met with even more attention. I seemed to get more attention there than most any other place in the world. I am not unaware that this is a multilayered phenomenon. I am not interested in drawing much attention to myself as I receive more than I would hope for. I am already seen as someone to be sold things to and be pestered if not hounded by beggars and the occasional scammer. I am none to bothered by the good folk seeking to sell me things, but it is only smart to be prepared for those few who are not so good. One of the main factors for this attention generally is from merely being a westerner, thus I am considered to have more money and hassled quite often so as to relinquish some of it. But another factor is undoubtably the color of my skin. I realize sticking out is not always a positive thing. Most people, indeed, are good, but it is not unreasonable to keep one's guard up in a place like India. I can assure you I never felt threatened, but to be made aware of such incidental things throughout the day is often unsettling, and can lead the mind astray.

Never have I been met with so many questions about my skin, people reaching out to touch my bare forearms, been asked so often to take pictures with so many random strangers or during common conversation had people comment on the color of my eyes and hair. I realize many things in these instances.

Primarily that I am a foreigner in this land. Another being that this affects others in some way. At first, I find it perverse, but a common characteristic of poor and isolated places is a lack of diversity that manifests itself in such inquiry and interest. Inexperience with other races and cultures is often a cause for base curiosity.

Since there is a Caste system in India, it is best to consider that Indians are more or less forced to see the world through skin color, and to understand that overcoming such a rigid cultural system is incredibly difficult. The Caste system is a profound and immovable reality of life in India, which for centuries has resulted in suffering and discrimination even though Indian society has come a long way in reducing its significance. However perverse the mentioning of race may be in a social setting, in India people are as blunt about it as they are about many things, and it often comes across as innocent. In the same way they talk about race they will ask if I am married or how many children I have. I realized it is all that some people have to discuss. It is a simple way of understanding, an unfortunate prism through which some view life. Race is something people think about as casually as they think about the weather. On my first visit, my companions and I were three very pale white people traveling through a land where everyone was not that. The color of one's skin does carry weight on the sub-continent. There is historically, presently and likely always will be a perverse attitude towards race. People can be perverse when confronted with someone different. Call out the privileges of one's skin color or even the lack their of if you wish, but there is so often a perverse reaction when confronted by an other.

Of course, race is worthwhile to consider when traveling in India, but even more so one must also be conscious of gender. If I am to stress the presence of racial mindedness, then it is also right to stress the glaring disparity between men and women in Indian society. I am no psychoanalyst or sociologist, but it does not take much time to form an opinion on gender dynamics and sexuality in India. Without trying to sound too academic, I would say that the home of the Kama Sutra does not indeed have a very healthy culture regarding sex. Repression has consequences. This is a subject meant for the social scientists and academic researchers, but for a laymen like myself, the only way I wish to describe it as is non-Western.

There were a few instances when we were the victims of some small-time scams. Nothing very serious, but once you realize you have been scammed out of money and into going places, you further realize your ignorance and vulnerability in such a place. The attention we received was often overwhelming. At times the amount of staring aimed in our direction was enough to make us feel uncomfortable. Even though staring in India is often different than in the west and does not always have a negative connotation, it is a difficult distinction for a young person to make in a place so foreign and far away. I had an undoubtably different experience the second time I went to India. Traveling alone is much different than traveling with two pretty girls. While walking around the streets during both journeys I could not help, but conclude that the cause for so much attention the first time was the combination of race and gender. Being alone and older made the journey a more calm and less complicated experience. I had no time constraints and my only worry was myself.

Traveling is a kind of vanishing act. Some vanish into small town life, a job or a marriage while others vanish into another country. Traveling in India feels like vanishing from the west. The culture is all consuming, and it is necessary to make mental adjustments in order to get around and get by. Finding my way around is something I have become better at over time. Traveling with others made me realize that not everyone is meant to leave home. Being there for a second time made it easier to navigate the difficulties of travel in India. Much of the difficulty is in dealing with delays and crowds or people that won't stop trying to sell you something. I learned to enjoy being a foreigner. I learned to be more calm when confronted with the intensity of humanity in India, and accept it for what is.

My route to India the second time had several stops, Amsterdam for a few days, then to Istanbul where I ate Baklava and went to the five-hundred-year-old Cemberlitas Hammam, and the main hookah bar inside the Grand Bazaar. I smoked shisha with some Turks who knew a bit of English and we were able to laugh together for some time before parting. I flew to Kathmandu and wandered around the markets buying gifts to bring home and necklaces of orange flowers to admire for the few days I was in that messy city. I flew over Mount Everest, and while admiring it from the sky I felt no desire to climb it. It was of course covered in snow, and the thought of climbing it seemed absurd. It was beautiful and satisfying enough just to see and consider its immense size from above. It is surrounded by mountains not much smaller, but at one point this set of mountains abruptly ends and the land flattens out. This was India and the plane crossed over a snowy northern section of the country into Bhutan, a country that makes me happy just by thinking of it. I spent ten days there being guided around by a man named Sonam, because foreigners are not permitted to travel alone. Much of my days were spent at Buddhist Temples hearing about the ways of Buddhism as it is so intricate to the lives and society of the Bhutanese people. I went to countless temples, including the Fertility Temple, and Tiger's Nest which took about an hour to trek up to. The temples I enjoyed the most were rich in color on the inside, deep royal blues and fire-engine reds, along with rows of prayer wheels around the outside walls. One can delightfully see worshippers walking around the temples in a clockwise direction spinning each prayer wheel as they pray. I did this almost every day, enjoying the playful habits of Buddhism. It was peaceful, meditative and innocent. The ritual and repetitive movements were so physically and mentally soothing that it became inevitable to attain a cheerful inner peace. This is all enhanced by the smells of unique incense and butter lamps that burn at the altars amidst offerings from worshippers that include bowls of cream and cups of saffron water.

I bought colorful gifts, incense, prayer beads, and prayer strings to bring home. While I was there I experienced two small earthquakes, yet it was still one of the quietest countries I had ever been to with the most peaceful people on earth. During my last days in Bhutan I was both eager and anxious to be in India. When I landed in Delhi I was overcome by a wave of thought and confusing emotions. I had put so much into the month I had spent there when I was twenty-one-years-old. I used and thought about my experiences in India all the time up to that moment. It was a great part of the lense through which I had come to view the world, that is, with India in mind.

I started this journey in the north of the country in some places still unknown to me, firstly in the city of Amritsar in the heart of the Punjab. I was alone when I exited the airport late in the evening into a refreshingly cool climate. Arriving in this part of India at the end of January was decidedly different than my first arrival in the country. What was also noticeable was that no one pestered me for a taxi ride or tried to sell me things. It took me quite awhile to get a taxi, in fact. The people were eagerly waiting for friends and family to arrive while they let me and everyone else be. Just being alone was something I did not previously associate with India, because you are never really alone there, and it never lets you be, so much so that being crowded by people starts to feel like a quintessential part of life. It is as if India would tolerate anything except solitude. But Amritsar is not Mumbai nor is it Delhi nor Chennai. It is distinct in being the capital of the Sikh faith and its different and distinct culture is evident.

I was thrilled to be back in a place I had thought so often about returning to. It felt easy to be there, and I suffered no anxieties about what to expect. It was perfect to arrive in Amritsar at night, because it is inevitable to make your way down to the Golden Temple also known as Harmandir Sahib, the abode of God, which is the holiest place for Sikhs. A glorious and enchanting sight made all the better under a night sky. It is easy to be consumed with anticipation the closer one comes to the temple, because it becomes busier, the lights shine brighter, and the chanted prayers emanating from a sound system grow louder. Many of the small streets of the city are dimly lit and it appears that all light is focused upon the temple and the Holy Pool in which it sits. It is all a beautiful and brotherly scene. One need not be a Sikh to enjoy and partake in the life of the temple, because it is a scene of humanity and brotherhood even for those who are not of the Sikh faith nor know anything about it.

The temple complex is large and there are sections devoted to prayer and other religious duties, but what I enjoyed most was the giant food hall, Guru Kha-Langar, where anyone can eat for free. It is a never ending line of people. Masses of people from all over making their way inside while men hand out steel trays and bowls and spoons in rapid order. After entering the hall, a handler quickly sits everyone down on the floor in long rows facing other rows of people. There are probably ten rows of fifty people in each hall. Before you can even get settled on the floor, men with buckets scoop out food to you on your steel tray and then the bread man comes and drops two pieces into your hands. A young boy pushing a water cart comes along and opens up the spigot putting water into your steel bowl. It is quite a humbling scene amongst all those people, many of them poor, others perhaps not, sitting on the floor, eating the same food, doing as they do. They treat you well, and look at you as an equal. It brings you right on down to earth. It is impossible to not get along with those around and even more unlikely to not feel as though you are accepted by this community, this great mass of humanity.

When you are done, you drop your tray and bowl off at a large production line where they are to be cleaned and sorted by none other than the people who had just been eating off of them. It is not mandatory to take part, but giving a donation or cleaning around the facility is well appreciated. I did a bit of both and usually cleaned some trays for about half-an-hour. There are long troughs filled with soap and water and when you go up to one, a man cleans off your hands and then you start working alongside everyone. It is very loud as the trays are made of steel and everybody works very quickly. It is not hard to work at the same speed as everyone else, because there is a rhythm to it. You clean and scrub, and the trays and bowls never stop coming, there are always more trays to be cleaned. People never stop showing up to eat, the work is never done. I can imagine bringing my young nephews to such a place, to witness the humanity of another reality. I wonder how they would react to such a place. I wonder how I would have reacted to this scene as a child. In such a place I feel the wonderment and curiosity a child has when experiencing most anything for the first time.

I spent four days in Amritsar wandering around the Golden Temple complex, and around to various places across the city. I even went to the border ceremony in Attari, where Indian border guards do a ceremonial war dance with their Pakistani counterparts before shaking hands and closing the border gate each evening. The Indian side was full of spectators who boisterously cheered everything the soldiers did. The stands on the Pakistani side were half full, and they did not cheer as loud. It did not appear as important to them. It seemed as if they were told to be there. The Indian side was overflowing with cheering citizens and a handful of tourists, all shouting, "Hindustan!"

I left Amritsar and spent two days in the ghostly creation of Chandigarh. It is Le Corbusier's planned city for the capital of the state of Punjab. It was surreal, and as much as I like a lot of that boundary-breaking modern architecture, this really took it to the limits. Never have I seen so much concrete. The main government buildings are the most unique and somewhat photogenic, but Le Corbusier designed the entire city, and it is odd to think of this place as a city in India. It was eerie at night, and especially when the fog rolled in it looked apocalyptic. It seemed unimaginable that Indians would tolerate such a design in their country. I think one visit to Chandigarh was enough for me. It looked like a foreign land Indians had been exiled to. I could only think of how I wanted to go back to the India I had seen a couple days earlier.

I took the train south to the north of Rajasthan to the city of Bikaner. The train was nearly sold out and the only cars with any seats left were in third class. We left on time, but still arrived late. I slept little as a consequence of the impossibly loud snoring of other passengers and the frequent stops at stations with much noise coming from the platforms. I was in the top bunk and to stop the others from snoring for a little while I loudly hit the ceiling of the car twice and then quickly pretended to be sleeping. Everyone awoke and asked each other what was going on, even looking down the hallway for a suspect or a clue.

In my mind India was never cold, but I was proved wrong while traveling across much of the Punjab. I was not prepared for the frigid temperatures that leaked through the windows and doors of the train. The temperatures in Chandigarh had been moderate and only cool for about an hour in the morning. Even after we had crossed into Rajasthan at around three or four in the morning I was shivering in my thin cotton pants and ended up putting on every piece of clothing I had. At one long stop at a local station I bought cup after cup of Karak chai from a seller on the platform, trying to warm my body from the inside out. It was delicious and sweet and full of cardamom and star anise. I became just as eager for the taste as I was for the warmth. It was not until a few more hours further into Rajasthan that the temperatures steadily rose, the heat became strong and the wind that flowed through the train's open windows and doors was now decidedly warm. The landscape was now flat and dry. The sun was blindingly bright and the rays did not gilt anything it touched, rather it flattened everything, giving the earth a pale complexion.

I was happy to be far from the dystopian aura of Chandigarh and back in a more recognizable Indian landscape. Perhaps the state of Uttar Pradesh is the most Indian of all the states, particularly because of its sacred significance for Hindus, but if any other state is to come close it must be Rajasthan. I was familiar with Rajasthan and on my first visit had spent some time in two of its jewel-like cities. The magical lake of Udaipur with the palace at its center is something to admire and take home with you to contemplate forever. Above the shops and restaurants on small dirt streets were large monkeys causing all kinds of mischief. The city of Jaipur was nothing short of an architectural wonder and an explosion of color. And once again did I witness some even more mischievous monkeys at Hanumanji Temple where they were having a go at whatever they could get their hands on from the tourist's bags and pockets. There was a place in Rajasthan I had read about while I was there, but not able to make it to. I always regretted not visiting the Karni Mata Temple in the small town of Deshnoke. Even before arriving in the Punjab I had made a point of it to make my way to the temple before the trip was over.

Arriving in Bikaner felt familiar to other arrivals in Indian towns and cities I had experienced before. Immediately, I was met with a swarm of Tuk-Tuk drivers and soon enough I was speeding by trotting camels on a two lane road through the desert to Deshnoke. Though, I was unfamiliar with this route I was quite aware of what I was heading towards.

Hinduism is a complicated religion that is difficult for someone like myself to even attempt an explanation. But one characteristic is that there are many different gods, and they arise out of local feeling and tribute to something or someone that for one reason or another came to inspire devotion and faith. In the case of the Karni Mata Temple, the story goes that upon the death of a local prince he was reincarnated as a rat, and a temple was built in Deshnoke where rats became a symbol of idolatry and devotion. One of the results of this is a few thousand rats running around the temple.

I had wondered what this place was like for twelve years. Whenever I heard someone speak of India, I thought about how I had not been to Karni Mata. I was a bit nervous before going in and hesitated outside for a little while, talking to people and buying some colorful bracelets. I kept wondering if the rats would be aggressive and try to bite or run up onto me. I thought of the smells and other repulsive things I might encounter. The temple had a fort like structure with long walls that were painted in shocking-pink. Music and chants emanated from behind the temple walls and I was surprised to not see rats scurrying about out front.

I took my shoes off, but left my socks on and tiptoed through the entrance. There were about a hundred people casually sitting amongst the rats. They did not flinch if a rat ran over their foot or beside them. They were some of the calmest and most content people I have ever seen. Their contentment conveyed that there was no other place they would rather be.

There were people sitting on the floor feeding

them, sitting on the steps touching them, sitting on the ledges holding them. As they went to the shrine to make offerings and get blessings from the priest they were surrounded by rats, as they walked about the temple their paths were crossed by rats. Rats walk along every ledge, rats walk up and down the edges of doorways, rats squeeze in and out of every hole or crack in the temple walls, rats eagerly perch themselves on the edges of large shallow bowls filled with cream. Fifteen rats on each bowl rapidly drinking this offering from the worshippers.

I spoke to the priest of the temple, a man named, Gajandra, asking him a few questions and he had much to say. When I asked if he was from Deshnoke or Bikaner, he interrupted abruptly and said, "no I am from this place, this temple! I used to be a rat and now I am here, this is miracle." It was startling to hear such a unique proclamation. I could not laugh nor be disgusted, because of how serious he was. I stood there speechless and just accepted what he said before speaking of other things.

He was dressed unceremoniously. No long garb or robe and no oversized hat, just a pair of navy blue pants and a gray button down shirt, and his feet bare. This is what he wore to perform his duties at the center of the temple, which included him holding a large steel plate filled with flower petals and one or two rats while blessing the stream of worshippers that came in from outside. Another ritual included holding a pot with a flame burning inside. Worshippers would briefly hold their hands over it and then rub their palms on their face. Some young kids walked around playfully while holding a rat in their hands.

Before I go any further into the temple and the many places where rats could be found, I must express something to you. Do you know what a rat is? Do you understand the meaning of a rat? Surely everyone has their own personal opinions; significant, indifferent or otherwise, but there is generally a similar opinion across the world about the repulsive nature of rats. Coming from New York, a place where I have spent much of my life, you hear about rats in common conversation. You hear about it so commonly that rats are simultaneously villains and mascots of that city. Rats live amongst the people of New York perhaps more so than other places. It is not uncommon for most New Yorkers to have some sort of story about a rat; an interaction, a battle, a sighting, a horror story. Sometimes people even refer to their dealings with rats as war-stories. Coming up through the toilet, in the walls, in the kitchen, in the bed, running across your foot in the street, seeing many of them eating away at some pile of trash or just flattened on the pavement. There is always a hideous mystery to them in New York and when they are sighted, it is with horror we react at just how large they often are. I am reminded of Orwell's vivid descriptions of rats in *1984*.

The way a New Yorker says the word, rat, is different than anywhere else in the world. Nowhere else can it be expressed with such vitriol and hateful spirit. It sounds different than some continental Italian or Spaniard saying, rata, which lessens the vitriolic nature of the word.

The word, rat, has a particular meaning to us Americans and more so to those of us who have lived around New York our whole lives. It is not just representative of verminous chaos, but has been assigned to the character of a particularly low individual, a betrayer, the disloyal, the treacherous, a stoolie, the worst thing one could be. There is no label, no slur more vicious and personal than, rat. It is drenched in a deep seated hatred. A rat is hate. We hate a rat.

To experience rats is to be confronted with darkness, but then to witness rats in the loving hands of human beings who are enveloped in grace, I could not help, but consider them in a new light. At Karni Mata I saw them pick up those rats and hold them in their hands as delicately as if they were holding a Fabergé egg. And they love them. They genuinely love the rats they are holding in their hands and bring them to their chest to love them even more. I saw people holding rats, caressing them and it gave them immense joy.

At the sight of this love and affection for rats, I was forced to reconsider my idea of beauty. Still, I could not deny to myself the hideous aesthetic of the rats, but what was forever profound to my eyes was the beauty of the people's love for them. How could I completely consider them as ugly as I once did when all those people before me so clearly loved them. How could I go on thinking in the manner I had once thought before when I now knew that there was nothing in the world more important, nothing more sacred to these people than a rat. I realized at that temple that you could be looking at something clear as day, sure as could be, knowing that it is the ugliest thing there is, ever was, and would be, and that stigma of ugliness can disappear. The beauty was there, it was all around, it lived in understanding that those worshippers were made whole by rats. This is the other side of beauty.

My assumptions were shattered and I was able to find literal beauty in what I had witnessed. It was beautiful not merely because the worshippers found solace in it, but because like India itself it was a mirror in which one could reach transcendence and realize that the truest beauty of all comes in moments of understanding. Beauty is mostly something we see and feel, but one of the most beautiful things a person can experience is an understanding where it was once absent. Understanding has the ability to erase distance between people, countries and cultures. It has the graceful power to take something that is foreign and make it familiar. The ability of knowing someone or something that is distant brings us closer to completeness while we are still living. That is beauty at its most cerebral and profound.

As difficult as some things are to understand, there

are few things fully out of reach of comprehension. Wherever people are, others like to tell them that that is all they know. If one is poor they are told they do not know how to be in high places. If one is rich they are told they do not understand the sufferings of the unfortunate and the beleaguered. But I disagree with such hasty conclusion making of human beings. For a man is generally more complex than any circumstance. We have the capacity for knowing, we have the ability to understand, if we so shall choose.

I stayed at the temple for four hours and even got to see the lucky white rat. A man told me he has only seen it once in twenty visits. I had some pleasant conversations with some more of the worshippers and took pictures with some others. I left as the twilight broke into night, and the air was cool on the ride through the desert back to Bikaner, where I was to catch a train to Delhi. The desert looked unfamiliar without the sun, and the surreality of those few hours at Karni Mata put everything further back in my mind. I was in a talkative mood, and while waiting for my train I spoke with a group of young people for a couple hours.

I must thank you for giving me that five-word-phrase. I do not know if it is yours or it originates elsewhere, but I do not really care either way. I am just grateful that you gave it to me, because I now believe it is something I have been unconsciously seeking for many years. I cannot help, but tie these words generally to my experiences and thoughts of

India and its influence upon me. With those five words I am now able to give many things more words and gain a greater understanding.

Henry Miller wrote that, "the most wonderful opportunity which life offers is to be human." Karni Mata and India itself afforded me the opportunity for experiencing humanity in a unique way. One must realize that humanity is beautiful, even when it is confusing and unfamiliar and disgusting and violent and strange, humanity has the willingness and ability to endure, it attempts to make sense of reality despite the difficulties of existence. No matter how absurd or different a belief may be, it is a separation from the true beasts on earth.

I have found the other side of beauty, because I have found another kind of beauty. It is not just a function of aesthetics, but also another state of mind. When I experience such beauty that is paradoxical to my own idea of it, I can only think that it is good for me. It can only make a mind more beautiful. All of this travel and experience has taught me to be satisfied with the goal of making my mind more beautiful. A beautiful mind is equipped with a verbal arsenal, a wealth of knowledge, a cannon of opinion and a fruitful garden of aestheticism. I believe that when one gradually beautifies their mind, life around them will then become more beautiful.

Not only was Karni Mata a place of understanding, it was a welcoming atmosphere. I was the outsider in every way possible, and never was I asked if I believed as they did, nor was I told to leave for not believing as they do. I knew that I would not have been so welcomed in other places around the world. Not all faiths or cultures are entirely accepting of others. There are unfortunately tribal litmus tests in some places, often when they are religious.

Religion is impossible not to notice in India. Its relevance, its importance, its peculiar traditions and the culture it creates throughout India are profound. The traveler is inevitably confronted by this pillar of Indian society and responds to it in different ways. I remember on my first visit, admiring the Bodhi Tree in Bodhgaya, where the Buddha first became enlightened, and I saw Bhuddists from all over the world, meditating and praying nearby. There was also the peculiar sight of some dreadlocked Americans and Europeans pretending to take part in the ceremonies; trying to mimic the pilgrims around them without a true devotion to the faith.

It is odd to witness such people, for it is a phenomenon that seems to only go one way. It also appears to be evidence of a person lacking in identity. Rarely is there any depth to their character. Westerners of this type in India are nauseating because they possess a kind a dreamy attitude where they think nothing is ever wrong, all is perfect and inspiring all the time. It is easy to see how this can happen at places like Hindu temples as they are so different than the empty places of worship in the west. Their emptiness manifests in obsession and overly loving something that is new, while they often reject and blame every fault in the world on their own culture and their feeble character.

One must also consider the racial factor in the western experience of India. A lot of people simply start acting strange when they are around a different race of people, more so when they are far from home. This can be the result not just of ignorance, but also inexperience and insecurity. The westerner often has a guilt complex which they over compensate for by being quixotic about everyone and everything around them. What comes of their inspiration is usually a change in dress and the addition of an excessive amount of bracelets and necklaces, perhaps a nose ring, but rarely do they gain a deeply held devotion to a people and its culture. These are the same people that are always talking about empathy and sympathy and how terrible it is where they originate from. What good is sympathy without action? What good is empathy without the alleviation of suffering? Words like empathy and sympathy mean nothing without action and are merely words to emotionally intoxicate people who proclaim how much they care and who are merely in possession of a savior complex. People with nothing want neither sympathy nor empathy, they want to be left to be and they want to be free.

India is a good place to reveal an absurdity in the western perception, mainly the obsession with helping others who are far away rather than those who are nearby. The spirit of the Dickens character, Mrs. Jellyby, lives in many a western traveler. I always wondered why such travelers were never offering the same kind of help to people who live in Mississippi, Jaywick, Appalachia or the East End or even talking about the need to help the poor and beleaguered in such places. Many westerners arrive in India and other parts of Asia and Africa with a savior complex, and if they did not arrive with one, they often depart with one. What they fail to realize is the poor do not need the philosophies and the emotions of others. They do not need the empathy nor the sympathy of a passerby. The poor do not need to be understood. I found that no one in India nor anywhere else I have traveled for that matter wants sympathy nor empathy from some mawkish visitor, especially one who does not act upon such feelings. So often, such sentiments do nothing, but serve one's own emotions and further the cultural divide. These types of travelers are always cosmopolitan, supposedly liberal(whatever that means these days), guilt ridden, desperate to be perceived as open minded, all knowing and cultured. At its heart, this type of character is the antithesis of understanding.

I always try to step back from my experiences in India as much as possible, to separate myself from the surreality of the experience, to see it for what it was, and what its traditions, its people and its culture are. It is indeed quite easy to get caught up in the beauty of a place like Karni Mata and other temples, but never did I have the impulse to go native or try to be some temporary believer or savior of all who suffer in India. I have come to understand that it is important not to get too sentimental about a place like India, no matter how significant its impact may be. I recognize that it is important to not merely see the beauty of a culture, but to also recognize its flaws, and the consequences that arise from it traditions and beliefs. Every culture has blemishes, and with so much poverty around, one must consider all factors in a place like India.

I take note of this kind of visitor, because I find religious belief in India to be entirely genuine. It is not a part-time thing, it is interwoven into all of society. Practice of religion is something consistently done from birth until death almost without exception. Religion is different in western countries. In the west, religion is mere decoration for many, a remnant of childhood or tied to memories of something one's elders once were, which is not exactly evidence of a deep-seated faith. It is more of a choice or preference, whereas in India and much of Asia it is a duty and obligation necessary to remain part of a community.

Mark Twain said that, "America's religion is work." I find that to be mostly true, but I think that statement could be conjoined with the idea that Americans have a religious-like obsession with their standard of living. I say this, because as an American I am acutely aware of standard of living. Americans manage how they live down to a single degree in temperature in a room and thousands of other minute details that most go without. Which is why I say that no American can honestly go to India and not take note of the conditions the people are living in. Poverty is not unique to India, but in few other places is it so vast and bluntly presented to you. In every landscape, altitude, temperature, and setting; urban or rural. I must also confess that I find nothing of spiritual inspiration in India, because there I am confronted by so much poverty and despair. While my mind is satiated by the customs of spirituality, I cannot deny to myself the sufferings it causes and the suffering it neglects. I find the human factor to be too real to reject. Real religious faith is a way of life. True faith requires abiding by rules set down long before you by your predecessors. Real religion and true faith require sacrifice of many modern principles and material things that people in the west hold dear.

People find security in faith and solace in worship. This is commonly deemed a necessity of difficult circumstances. People are often stuck in the place and conditions they were born into for their entire lives. It takes immense effort, fortitude and often luck to overcome arduous beginnings. Belief and faith can only do so much for a person. Sometimes the mind can be detrimental to the body and a person can drown themselves in any belief, religious or otherwise. To live is to be amongst the abundance of reality, which brings about the humble practice of questioning one's own beliefs. Something like reincarnation is a grand promise for an unfortunate soul. But such a concept is an unfortunate rejection of the beauty that is now, and a dismissal of a human being that is here. To improve one's circumstances in life one must move beyond it with action that is applicable to their present state of being.

If you move and travel enough, and just keep on going, you can find a way to move beyond faith, and indeed find solace in the reality of life on earth. You can reach a state of humility and realize it is a mere necessity of understanding and when you stay in motion you will hopefully find that the most important state of being is amongst the multitude of humanity. Reality is the most significant thing to have faith in, because in its consequences there are only immovable truths. That is a moral foundation human beings can bend towards, that is a god worth facing.

I arrived in the city of Kochi, down south in the province of Kerala, nearing the end of my second visit. It had been a long, arduous, yet fulfilling journey that involved many delays and crowded train rides as is common when traveling around India. I kept thinking to myself with surprise and wonder of how I finally made it to Kerala. It, like many other places in India, had been a name I had been thinking about since I first visited twelve years before. I had been wanting to come back to India ever since I left that first time, and Kerala was one of the places most important for me to see

The anticipation of arriving in a place after twelve years is bound to leave one with some sort of a let down. But it was a let down born out of an illusion of my own making, for I had no idea what to expect on arrival. All I ever knew about Kerala was that it was very green, and populated by far fewer people than any other state in India. It being less dense than most every other state in India was interesting to me in and of itself. Still, I foolishly thought it would mirror my arrival in other Indian cities and towns, which often involved the presence of thousands of people who populate the train stations for the multitude of reasons one is at a train station. Kerala's main station of Ernakulam, was a deserted place. As I walked from the station to the small port to catch a boat to Kochi, I could only ponder the equally deserted streets. It was not a let down, as I had previously felt with the station, but simply the arrival in a quiet place; and a quiet place can take time to acclimate to just as it takes time to acclimate to a noisy metropolis.

I had always felt Kerala was a kind of lush oasis, a relieving and less populated part of India that could only have a resoundingly different character as a result. I formed the idea that Kerala was a paradisal place and never ceased to imagine how deeply green and lush it would be. It was certainly different than all of India's megacities I had visited.

As I sat in a park beside my hotel sipping a cold tea, the fantasy, my fantasy, of Kerala slowly began to fade and I was met with one of India's harsh realties. There are few places in the country that are absent of sweltering heat, the only real difference from one place to another is the form in which it takes. In the case of Kochi, it was intensely humid. Like somewhere in the Deep South of the United States in summer, but even more so and year round. This is one of the things that a person en route to India may think is simple enough to deal with, but when faced with such relentless and unforgiving heat, one realizes it is a constant confrontation that puts demands on a mind already faced with an unfamiliar setting. Even being near the beach and in the 'winter' month of February it was physically uncomfortable to stay outside during the hottest hours of the day. A casual walk takes a peculiar amount of effort, and is oddly taxing. The sun is powerful, and you are aware of it more than anywhere else on earth. Though, Indians in Kerala do not seem to notice the sun or the heat radiating from it, they are used to it, perhaps many have never experienced it any other way.

I know, I allow myself to complain about the heat, but I did not let it stop me from seeing Kerala and living my life. Wasting time is an unforgivable sin. If it is too much, then it is best to just leave, and so I stayed. I purposefully woke up very early some days in order to walk a bit without the heat of the sun. One morning, from the center of Kochi I walked south to one of the most interesting places I had visited in all of India, the nearly five-hundred-year-old Paradesi Synagogue. It is without worshippers these days, for the town, which is literally called Jew Town, and basically all of southern India is bereft of its former Jewish population. It was never a large community to begin with, but it existed nonetheless. The history of Jews in Kerala is one that locals understand the importance of, not merely as a magnet for tourists, but for its rarity and fragility in that part of the world. The fact that a synagogue is protected and cared for by Indians of different faiths is a touching and pleasant happenstance. This is one of the beauties of Kerala, its incredible diversity and acceptance of others. On my walk to the synagogue I also stepped into a boisterous and music filled service at a Catholic Church. There is hardly a place in India not consumed with religious belief, even in Kerala, one of its more secular states.

My journey south continued to Alapuzzha which is often shortened to Aleppey, to see its canals. The heat only increased the further south I went. The canals were not as charming as I had imagined, and were long stagnant pools littered with overgrown vines and unfortunately some trash. There was hardly a boat moving through the wide waterways. The ones that could be seen were docked in some seemingly random spot and the canals looked more like an abandoned industrial endeavor. Still they were painted in a satisfying yellow, which contrasted nicely with all the overgrown greenery beside it. People preferred to move about on the noisy streets with motorbikes and Tuk-Tuks. The beach was massive, but difficult to enjoy because of the heat. So I moved further south to Kollam and spent five days near the beach in Varkala. I stayed on the cliff most of the time and only was I able to venture down to the beach around five in the afternoon when the heat and force of the sun had somewhat subsided. It was always around one-hundred-degrees Fahrenheit when I went in the water and I had to wear a hat and t-shirt to protect myself from the sun.

There were a few Hindu temples nearby and I was surprised by what I am usually surprised by at these temples, which is the way in which they worship. Hinduism is a peculiar religion for its local eccentricities from one place and temple to another across India. There are many Gods in Hinduism that take shape in various forms. There are temples where the symbols or object of worship can range from airplanes to snakes. At one temple near Varkala, there were dozens of plastic baby dolls strewn about and hanging from a tree, and these were considered some kind of religious symbolism. They were modern dolls for children and could not have been there for more than a couple years. I wondered how often they were changed or if it was a new symbol. When I visited this temple, I could hear very loud and worrying noises nearby. Like gunshots or small bombs, the sound would go off every few minutes. When I walked passed another temple I found that the noise came from large fireworks set off as an offering to the temple and their god. Worshippers would give five or ten Rupees and the man working there would set off a small or large firework according to how much the worshipper paid. I watched a few worshippers take part, and each time had to cover my ears at the incredibly loud bang. It was a peculiar yet wildly entertaining sight. I was compelled to take part and several times did I hand over ten Rupees to the man who insisted on waving the little explosive over my head in a circular motion several times, before walking to his small demolition area to set it off. The expression on his face never changed the entire time. He was performing a serious duty,

After Varkala I made my way further south to Thiruvananthapurum, often shortened to Trivandrum, for a few days before spending some time in Sri Lanka. My first journey to India was a circular route around the country and the second was a southerly journey that started in Amritsar, in the northern state of Punjab. India is a large country and there is so much of it that is considered to be the south. On my way to Kochi I tried to go to a picturesque hill-top town called Ooty, which has thankfully been shortened from Udhagamandalam, but it was too much of a trek via bus or taxi. I think eight hours in total from which I would have had to backtrack the same distance before getting the train to Kerala.

I was already far south when I made the decision to get the sleeper train after three days in Tiruchirapalli, which is thankfully nicknamed Trichy. Most of my time there was spent at the Sri Ranganathamswamy Temple, I was unable to locate its nickname. The sun was as hot as the names of these cities are long. It was a pleasure to take in the peculiarities and grace of the people who walk about as well as all the colors of the whole complex that sits on an island between the Kollidam and Kaveri Rivers. An ancient place, full of brightly colored clothing, flowers and temples, all packed tightly together, baking in the heat of the sun.

Amidst the temple complex, on a street corner, there was a man sitting atop an elephant. Passersby would put some money into the end of the elephant's trunk and then be blessed by the elephant giving a gentle tap on the head with its trunk. The blessed went on their way while the elephant stretched his trunk backwards to the man sitting atop who would pocket the money. This happened as quickly and effortlessly as a handshake with a friend passing in the street. Being confronted by the presence of an elephant on the street is not a surreal or unusual thing in India, just for those visiting. I made sure to get a blessing from the elephant, and I was delighted when the great mammal tapped his trunk on the top of my head.

India is both enlightening and dumbfounding. Perhaps one could say this about many countries. In Trichy, I had a few hours to kill before getting on the night train. It was loud everywhere inside the station so I went out front where it was quieter. I sat on the ground and leaned up against the wall of the front of the station thinking I had found a peaceful spot when a policeman came up to me, waved his nightstick in my direction and said I could not sit nor loiter there. I got up and walked a few feet to where I saw an old man, who I am quite sure was dead on the ground. Flies and all. The pack of policemen could see him, too, occasionally giving a long stare, yet they continued to shoo away idlers. It was a difficult thing to experience even though it was not the first dead person I had seen in India. I have seen the dead in similar situations in other countries, but it is something I never get used to. This man's body made me feel that death is always near in India, and what bothered me more than death itself was the indifference of the living.

I have heard people make the case that war is beautiful, and this is always a difficult concept to accept. It is a stretch of a statement and of the imagination, but sometimes we must think in and look at the dark corners of life to understand that there is indeed light in such places. Beautiful occurrences do arise as a result of grim circumstances. I had seen three dead people on the side of the road in three weeks. No one made a fuss, no one did anything about it nor did an ambulance arrive. It was sad to see, of course, and I was forced to think of death more vividly. There is so much death in India that life feels completed all around. Since death was often in the air and plain to see, I sometimes wondered if it was okay to acknowledge or consider that death is beautiful, too. Simply because it is a person's last act, their final state. We know there will be suffering and for many of those sufferings that human beings are susceptible to, the remedies are so often out of reach or sadly rejected, yet people talk about the beauty of the poor, the righteousness of poverty, and the humility of hardship. So I feel inclined to state that there, too, is something beautiful in death.

Twelve years earlier I watched bodies be cremated into the Ganges River at Varanasi. There were many people around, casually and peacefully watching the end of a few men's lives, and the so-called continuation of life's circle. I tried to look upon those dead men in the street in a similar fashion even though they were far from that holy river. When you see a dead man, the instinct is to look away, out of respect and decency, also to not be horrified or traumatized by such a dreadful circumstance. But I glanced and I looked, thinking that it showed the man some amount of respect. I tried to recognize the beauty of his life, that he had been alive, and his life was now complete. Time seems slow-moving in India, and in those moments of awakening when one looks at a dead body on the street, in the moments of revelation, in one's encounters with beauty; you realize that time is indeed real, and it exists in all things.

Miguel de Unamuno's *The Tragic Sense of Life*, is a book and a phrase I could not remove from my mind when I was in India. Perhaps I am looking too closely, thinking too much, but I sought to stay in the moment, here on earth, in India, without delusions. I keep my tragic sense of life close-by, because so often the truth of many things in life is that they are tragic. To witness the suffering of others is not to know it completely, but to gain an understanding, which if nothing else, provides a few ounces of clarity. To witness an expired body is not nothing, it is something. The sight of a dead man in the street leaves a mark on the conscience. I do not say it is beautiful in and of itself, but those men I saw on the street, lifeless and gone, were human beings, and I knew there once was happiness in their life in some way. They will never come again, but at least they have been.

I was hanging around the market in the center of Trichy when some police officers asked me what I was doing there. "This is dirty place," one of them said, and encouraged me to go to some upscale hotel nearby. I told them I did not mind where I was, and indeed I liked where I was at. I sat with some locals drinking coffee which they would pour out of a small brass pitcher held at shoulder height while the cup was held down below the waist. When the cup was full, the height of each would quickly reverse and the coffee poured back into the pitcher, this was repeated three or four times before being served. In the sweltering heat a small group of people would watch and passersby would pause briefly to watch one or two pours. You see pretty little scenes like this all over India, people going about their day in interesting ways. You do see scenes of life going well, and in Trichy I saw many families eating together, mothers carrying babies, groups of people laughing over some tea. All is well in some places. But when you leave the market or the nice hotel, and you turn the corner you are confronted with a kind suffering that cannot really be understood or dealt with. You see millennial and inescapable poverty, something that will never change.

Trichy does not have as many people living on the street as megacities like Mumbai and Kolkata, but you still see people on the street that have never had anything, not even a chance. You see one and then another and then it gradually multiplies and as you see more people living on the street in destitution they take up space in your mind and the people start to lose their individuality. You do not see them clearly anymore. You see them as being a part of a condition that exists. You realize you cannot save them, you try to help, but you yourself cannot save everyone. The impulse is to save, to help, to heal, and this impulse is defeated by the grim realities of the situation. It is important to feel and know this, because it is the antidote to a savior complex, which tends to hurt more than help the persons meant to be saved. You see people who have nothing, and you begin to accept that they will always have nothing.

Before I was in Trichy, I had spent a few pleasant

days in the seaside city of Pondicherry, a well ordered and gridded city formally a part of French colonial territory. It appeared that not much had changed since the French had left, as it still very much resembled a seaside city or town in France. You asked me where I stay while I am here, and funny enough Pondicherry was the only place I had difficulty in finding a hotel for when I arrived at the one I had booked for a couple nights, had indeed been closed for some time. A woman working at the neighboring hotel confirmed this with a smile on her face at my surprise. I had to wander around before finding a room at a nearby ashram, which had basic rooms and plenty of rules, such as no visitors and the doors being locked between ten at night and six in the morning. I did not mind as I had been falling asleep early anyway.

Pondicherry proved to be pleasantly different than most any other part of the country. It was Indians living amidst the charming designs and remnants of French colonial planning. Unlike Chandigarh, this seemed a success of European influence on the sub-continent. It was a peaceful place where I was able to write much, including the last few paragraphs of my first book. For that alone I will always remember Pondicherry.

Though, I am never entirely used to this weather, I remain familiar with it, and conscious of how it plays a part in shaping the reality of each place in India. The seaside breeze in Pondicherry provided a welcomed break from the extreme heat, but Chennai was just as hot as Kerala and Trichy. In fact, Chennai may have been the most sweltering and unappealing city I have been to in all of India. It has a beautiful fort, but there is hardly a definitive face to that large metropolis. I love its previous name, Madras, which is still given to its coffee, but as a name for the city it has been flung out, like the British. Though, the presence of the British remains in small ways. Mostly at memorials, churches, museums and undeniably from the fact that English is spoken by many. It was difficult not to think of the British while in Chennai. The countless amount of people who left their cool and rainy island for a place that is so incredibly opposite is something I find fascinating. There were of course countless motives for venturing to the sub-continent, many of which were inspired by greed and other condemnable ambitions, but I think the impulse for so many people to go to India over the course of centuries can primarily be born out of a sense of adventure, a love of place and a deep desire to see oneself in that place. Something I can relate to. By being in India, I get to see myself in India. How I am, how I react, how I get on with life. Being out of your natural environment and out of your comfort zone forces you to look at and learn about yourself.

I sat at a temple in Chennai observing the worshipers amidst some of their strange practices, one involving a man slamming half a dozen coconuts into a large concrete circle. I got to talking with a man at the temple and when I told him I was from America he eventually said that everybody in America cares too much about money. As we spoke some more, I told him all the places I had recently been to and had been to in the past. He looked at me in amazement saying, "my friend how have you been to so many places like this?" I told him that, "money plays a part in it, money plays a part in getting me to those places and having those experiences, and I guess money brought me here to you today to tell you that."

After India, I spent ten days in Sri Lanka witnessing the mass of pilgrims at the Temples of Anuradhapura, along with the great rock of Sigiriya. Then it was a few stops in the Middle East. Kuwait where I laughed and made jokes with some Iranians who ran a restaurant in the main Bazaar, and then Qatar, where I hung out in the Falcon Souq and had a few of those majestic birds stand on my arm. I then stopped in Switzerland for a few days, and did very little other than admire the Van Gogh paintings at the Kunsthaus Zurich. I landed in New York City a few days before a large party was to be given by a dear friend to celebrate my birthday.

You once told me that I am blessed. After seeing all these places in such a short period of time I cannot help, but agree. Your questions are important to me and gave me the energy for reflection and contemplation. It makes me feel blessed to have been able to speak of all these things to you. I hope your curiosity has been satisfied now that you can see all of which I was among.

The people and the rats of Karni Mata will never leave me, just like the scenes of that perilous street of a Mumbai slum. The problems of the poor in India stay with me. I am incapable of forgetting the conditions I have seen, and they will forever shape me. I learn from it, simply to not complain about anything, but also to keep a sensible perspective of reality, to not worry about much, because in the castle of the United States compared to the castle of India, there is much less to worry about.

I look back at the route I took, the things I saw, the people I met, I contemplate all the thoughts that come to my mind and I am filled with joy for everything I possess, most of all, my experiences. I am indeed blessed, I have everything, certainly I have my time in India, which continues to provide and teach me how to look at and deal with the world. Perhaps, at times I have lofty visions of that country, but what I have come to believe is indeed tied up in India's earthly existence. It is special to me, because it will always be foreign and unreachable, and it will always feel like a brief encounter. I have gained so much from that distant land. I think of my younger self and all the mistakes I made, all the moments of culture shock and revelation. With each revelation there was a cerebral shift. Deep experiences force such things about, altering me for all time. The light falls upon my ignorance.

There is a drama that comes with the first realization of getting older. It is a profound moment, like reaching the end of a bridge that once appeared to have no end.

India has done that for me. It has provided me with a mirror to not only look at my own country and culture, but to look at myself. Fortunately, I was provided with this mirror the first time I went to India. I not only see myself in India all those years ago, but I see how much I have changed since. I see how much I have changed as a result of having been in India, and what those experiences have continually given me to this day. I realize how lacking I might be were it not for those days under an Indian sun. I experienced another state of mind, made possible by beauty of another kind. Those days were beautiful.

Beauty has its place in life, find it where you will, I found it in India. I might not have found it had I not taken that first journey all those years ago, and the same can be said for the second journey. It is important to meet people where they are. That is why going to places is important, and going back to them is, too. Returning to a place like India provides perspective on a culture that is more complex than nearly anyone or anything on earth. It is a perspective I have become a part of. One in which I am not only able to see India as it was and is, but I am now able to see myself in a similar light. I understand that of the many things that India is, it is a teacher. And it can teach all manner of things to a traveler. Therefore, it was not until coming home from this second journey that India made me look back on my former self and understand that I had everything to learn.

Harar

If you are prolific enough in your travels, your reasons for doing so will start to evolve in ways that more suit your intellectual needs rather than the simple pleasures afforded by a nice Caribbean beach or a charming Alpine village. Experience can lead to more eccentric curiosities, dare I say kinks. Some seek out religious relics, ancient ruins or mountains to climb while others plunge into a black hole of hedonism. Those are all delightful endeavors, but with all the time I have spent with the words of some writers I often feel inclined to pay a visit to a place which contributed to their story. A literary pilgrimage perhaps, but mostly to walk in the shoes of a creative mind and to get a sense of how their eloquent words came to be.

I have looked upon gravesites, places of birth, and plaques stating the years that this man lived here from this year to that year. I have read whole books about literary pilgrimages, people tracing the steps of Bruce Chatwin, Graham Greene, and George Orwell among others. All with delight I turned those pages about writers I myself admired and in my own way retraced some of their routes in order to investigate their mindset. I recently passed through Lowell,

Massachusetts and saw the gravesite, house and a park named after Jack Kerouac. There is not much other reason to stop in Lowell for it is a sad place with the same characteristics of many other forgotten towns, not just in New England or America, but anywhere else a place may be forgotten. A person has to come from somewhere, and that is where Kerouac was brought up and now rests after a wild and prolific literary life that means something to many people near and far. As proud as some Lowellians may be of its most famous son, there is more to life than a fast-living writer, but the fact that a man like Kerouac originates from there will always make Lowell a special place to his admirers. Bob Dylan supposedly sneaks into the graveyard on Kerouac's birthday for a few drinks and a smoke with his friend. Lowell may not mean much to most people, even to those who live there, but artists have a way of establishing meaning where it was once absent. That is why people consistently travel from afar to leave cigarettes, whiskey bottles, and other paraphernalia beside the gravestone of a man in Lowell, Massachusetts.

I admired Kerouac's story more than his writing, but a writer who I admired both for his story and his writings was Arthur Rimbaud. I had read nearly every published word of Rimbaud along with several biographies and essays of his life and work. So much so that I started to feel his influence in my restless traveling life. Restless and always wanting to leave. Leave, what?

It does not really matter. Some stories, some books are so good they can initiate a multitude of desires. The literary pilgrimage I often wished to take was a small gesture, in fact it was an insufficient sojourn in the quest for something of Rimbaud, the premier enfant-terrible, the rebel of all rebels, the master-walker, the professional wanderer, the ultimate drop-out. Another way to describe him is as the man who gave the most resounding fuck-you to literary life, domestication and art itself. That is the man I admired, identified with, wished I knew and was inspired by.

I had been wanting to go to Ethiopia ever since I read about Rimbaud, who lived the last ten years of his life in voluntary exile in the eastern Ethiopian city of Harar. The sheer randomness of this place was fascinating to me, much more so because Rimbaud comes from the small provincial city of Charlesvilles-Mézières in northern France tucked up against the border of Belgium. It always seemed like a mad thing to have done and I was perplexed when contemplating the length of time this young man spent in a culture so foreign to his own during a time when there was little in terms of finding ways to communicate and get on. What kind of person does such a thing? For one, it was a man who had written some brilliant poetry by the age of twenty-one and was admired throughout Parisian literary society until he made such a mess of his social and love life that it dissuaded many from liking him as a person. He rejected everyone and everything and fled from what he deemed the bullshit and pretentiousness of art and life in Paris. I think of Rimbaud's time in Harar as perhaps the greatest rejection of one's previous life there has ever been. Not just because of what he rejected, but also because of where he fled to. He rejected all that was near and simply preferred to be elsewhere. He rejected his old life. He was a man permanently in revolt.

If you read enough you might start to think you can know a writer just from their books. That connection can seem as real as one with a living person whom you have known personally, because you never know anyone completely. You can get closer to them, but there are always gaps in your understanding of another human being. I tried to a degree to know Rimbaud as much as I could. I thought him to be a rare person worth knowing better. I read all of his works and most of the biographies of him, especially Edmund White's *The Double Life of a Rebel*. On a trip to France I made a point to detour to Charleville-Mézières so I could see the town that this young man so often fled from and returned to. A town he referred to in scathing terms for its boring and bourgeois-ways. His house and the museum devoted to him stand as memorials to his life, both capable of leaving a mark on any faithful reader of his verse. But even before I walked up the stone steps to the museum, I knew I could get nowhere near understanding this man unless I journeyed to another place. That place was Harar, Ethiopia. He spent ten years there, but his life did not end in Harar. He found out he had cancer in his knee of all places and knew that his time was limited. He made the treacherous journey across the desert to the Gulf of Aden, and was able to sail back to Marseille where he died a few months later after having his leg amputated to try and impinge the spread of the cancer. He was a year younger than Van Gogh, and died a year after the painter committed suicide in France, both at the age of thirty-seven. A sad and strange end to a rebellious life.

Washington D.C. to Addis Ababa was a one way route I never considered, in fact, I never think much of anything that begins or ends along the Potomac. My mind is firmly settled along the Hudson, when it comes to much of America. At the moment, the only other river I sought to be near was the Nile. It was not such a drag to be tired and jet lagged in Addis Ababa, because it is kind of a drag of a city. The Ethiopian capital is an absurdly spread out place that is defeating to try and navigate on foot. You are forced to hail a taxi every time you want to do something. It reinforced my belief that the urban metropolis is an alien concept forced upon the African continent. It comes from the west and the east, neither of which Africa is naturally connected with. The African continent is south central. The strength of African civilization is in its rural character, because of its closeness to nature. Since there was no nature nearby, the best thing to do was drink delicious coffees and lattes from glass cups little bigger than a shot glass at Tomoca in the neighborhood gracefully named, Piazza. While Addis Ababa did little for me, sitting in this cafe for a few days was pleasureful. I had heard much about coffee in Ethiopia, and had drank it from time to time in other parts of the world. But the Tomoca brand was exceptional, decidedly strong and addictive.

After excessive caffeine consumption I took some time to admire the Cathedral of St. George and speak with some of the worshippers and others loitering like myself. At Holy Trinity Cathedral there were armed guards patrolling the complex, which included the Tomb of Haile Selassie, who is a fascinating ruler when you know nothing about him. There is a flair and mythical aura that surrounds him in life and death. At first I became enthused by the seemingly mythical Selassie, but after finishing a few biographies of him I realized how undeserving he is of such adulation. His divine status was solidified in his lifetime not just for being crowned Emperor, but also from being declared God-on-earth by the creators of Rastafarianism. He was a symbol of African power and autonomy throughout the continent and among the African diaspora in the western world. His ceremonial fashion and unique visage played a part in the strange admiration he garnered from western minds and fervent souls who wish to look up to a leader other than their own. His power began to wain in the last two decades of his life, and gradually his support started disappear.

In order for a monarch to maintain control and pass power on to an heir, it is necessary for it to have a mass of believers. Belief is a part of power. With the rise of another religion called Communism, Selassie's reign came under attack and was ultimately replaced just as his life came to an end. Selassie's mistakes were many and one of them was falling out of favor with the United States at a time when the Soviet Union was fomenting revolution at every corner of the continent. His reign was one of the last of its kind in Africa and the world. Though, monarchy often finds a plethora of faithful worshippers it is also necessary to repress any and all dissent. Selassie did much of this, but ultimately the communist forces grew too strong and those once loyal to him saw that his time was limited. The man deemed to be a God-on-earth had lost the faith of his once-loyal-subjects.

Selassie's allure has subsided in recent years. Young people simply do not know him. Monarchies do not work or seduce people as they once did. This is evidenced by how few of them remain on earth. The young and old alike have found other earthly gods to worship. The sovereignty he represented is often dismissed today because of his lavish style in a country and on a continent enveloped in famine, poverty and war.

Ultimately, Selassie became too moderate, too comfortable and too old to maintain his grip on power in a nation rapidly evolving in its character and under the relentless threat of international communism. He did not act fast enough to repress the communist challenge. In the end he was simply not brutal enough.

History has a strange tendency to forgive and minimize the brutality of monarchs and dictators, which sometimes leads to rulers of this sort finding admirers in the future. It may even lead to them having the words, 'the Great,' added to their name. People look back on all kinds of brutal leaders in admiration. Stalin and Lenin are still given favorable reviews from people in and outside of Russia today. Fidel Castro always had a legion of supporters around the world. But it is difficult to praise a man that loses control of his Kingdom. Such men are relegated to a sad corner of history. The essence of a monarch is power. A monarch is not meant to be moderate, especially on the African continent. It comes across as incompetence or indifference, both of which are deadly to the business of monarchy. To be conquered from within is evidence of great folly and ineptitude. In the business of power, brutality is a foregone conclusion, especially when the divine aura has begun to fade.

Addis Ababa is a city like most any large metropolis on the African continent. It exists more out of administrative necessity, as a center of power and commerce rather than as a center of culture. An ugly and confused layout is the result. Sub-Saharan Africa constantly fails at producing cities that one can admire in the same way they admire Tokyo, Paris or even something more recent like Dubai. Walking as a matter of leisure cannot really be done as everything is so spread apart. There is always the sense of walking through a parking lot from one business building to the next. A pedestrian is isolated and not accompanied by the cultural doings of people. The streets are nearly all boulevards and treacherous to cross amidst speeding cars and a blinding sun.

Soon enough I was in the northern city of Lalibela, which is jewel-like and its isolated location was a relief from the urban drudgery of Addis Ababa. The roads were terrible, but the scenery was satisfying. Roads are not a high point of traveling around Ethiopia, and thankfully it is easy to fly around the country to cover the long distances. Air travel is a kind of freedom in all African nations. Roads are a reminder of the endless faults of governments on the continent. The poor conditions make for slow going and can lead to accidents. Roads stretch through vast deserted areas making it a risky mode of travel, for there is always the possibility of some nefarious character putting up make-shift-tolls and demanding a bribe in order to pass. Americans are spoiled for roads. There is not really a better place on earth where roads are so vast, well maintained and seemingly stretch to every conceivable corner of the country.

The rock-hewn churches of Lalibela are a charming sight that satisfy a youthful impulse to create by digging into the earth. I looked down on the Saint-George church and thought of a child with a small shovel and bucket at a beach. It is surreal to look downwards at a building. It was pleasant to see that beautiful architecture can come about by reaching down and carving out the earth. It is both natural and man made. The design is so concise it is possible to forget that it is made of earth. Man's relations with earth do not always have such a beautifying effect. This was clearly the careful work of man, but done with faithful respect for the earth.

I was able to be present for some of the services inside the churches. Men were wrapped in white robes and had cloth wrapped around their heads like a turban. There were drums and bells, but much of the music was created from the rhythmic chants and songs emanating from the group of men pressed tightly together in the small space of the church interior. It was a thousand-year-old church and it seemed as though the songs and services had never changed. It was a beautifully ancient scene. Streaks of light came through the two windows carved out on the side. When the service let out it was a beautiful scene of men and women sitting together in their elegant robes under the sun. A women walked around with a large plate of bread, handing out a piece to everyone. This was markedly different from life in Addis Ababa. I could see the community that religion provided for everyone in this remote and humble place. It was a place untouched and uncorrupted by the devils of modernity.

While Lalibela was full of religious tradition and customs, the few days I spent in Axum revealed an even more spiritual side of Ethiopia. Religious sentiment abounds everywhere in Ethiopia and Axum is just as religious a place as Lalibela. Devotion is strong and the faithful are present in places of worship. The biggest difference between Lalibela and Axum was the style of churches.

I tried to visit the small building that supposedly holds the Ark of the Covenant, but the gates were locked shut with a posted sign proclaiming that only Ethiopians were allowed inside. I appealed to a security guard, but he was not interested in a discussion. Though, nearby there was a little museum of sorts. He undid an ancient lock on the door and it squealed open. It felt more like a storage room than a museum. It was small and cluttered with a couple layers of dust. There were personal items belonging to Haile Selassie and other former Kings and Queens, and gifts given from other nations. The guard walked me around pointing out instruments, saddles and toys that were over a hundred years old. Gifts from Russia, Britain, France and elsewhere all sat there just like junk in someone's attic. They were all interesting to see, but it was like witnessing the remnants of an abandoned empire.

A couple-hundred-meters away from the museum was a wooden sign nailed to a tree proclaiming in yellow letters, both in English and Amharic, "Remark

Women are not allowed into the Monastery Church."
The Fourth century monastery, The Old Church of Our
Lady Mary of Zion had a humble design and when
I knocked on the door it was soon opened by a little
man dressed in yellow robes and a circular yellow hat,
holding a long stick. His short stature and narrow
frame were welcoming. His unique face was young, but
I sensed he was much older than he looked. He had the
body of someone who had spent a lifetime fasting and
never consuming anything unnatural or detrimental to
his health. We were able to communicate through the
beauty of the walls of the quiet church. His voice was
hoarse and words always came forth with a gasping or
whispering sound. He immediately started to guide
me around, sometimes pulling my sleeve like a child
showing off his room. He moved a bench away from
a wall to reveal a beautiful painting of Mary. Then we
went to another wall and he tapped an image with
his stick and said, Joseph. He pulled aside some large
curtains to reveal a wall of paintings and pointed out
each biblical character. We did this with a few more
images of both Mary and Joseph and then with Jesus.
The religious paintings were beautiful. The eyes of
which were exaggerated and almost caricatures of
Ethiopian facial features. The walls of the church were
beaming with color. Bright yellows, greens and reds
depicting biblical scenes in a style I had never seen
before. The style was youthful and at times playful
to the eye and sensibility of anyone viewing these

images. Any section of wall that was not painted was the color of pale stone.

At the modern Church of Our Lady Mary of Zion there were plenty of worshippers, many of them women. Some sat slumped over on the pews dressed in layers of white sheets, while others lie sprawled out on the floor with their arms stretching out towards the altar. They were not resting, they were prostrating in reverence and devotion to god. Chanting and wailing in a submissive tone, overcome by belief.

I had walked passed another church nearby, where there were several dozen women on the ground outside in the same position. I could hear their collective chants from a hundred yards away. It sounded like they were in agony, and the looks on their faces were stressed. They were all older, from their demeanor and actions they looked even older and close to death.

People looked in pain, even though they sought to surcease from sorrow through religious practice. The intensity of the religious scenes was taxing. It was a lot to consume and comprehend in just a few hours time. Each person's face was significant and unforgettable. It felt like walking through a dozen museums and trying to appreciate thousands of works of art all at once. It was somewhat extreme, but it was also beautiful at the same time. I asked myself, what is this place? And I asked myself, what am I doing here? I soon knew the answer to both, because I admired the beauty of this culture that I walked among. It was a land entrenched in faith. The people entirely genuine about their faith. It was beautiful to witness something that had been happening unchanged for hundreds of years and would likely remain so for hundreds more. I immediately realized how brief and rare my encounter was with these people. The words I wrote, the pictures I took are all well and good reminders of that time. But to have seen and felt such a place has only left me feeling immeasurably rich.

There was not a tourist in sight. No other western faces. No westerner had the idea to go to Axum. Just me. I walked down a street of shops buying some colorful souvenirs. My favorite being fly swatters made of horse-hair attached to the end of a small stick. In my sight nearly the whole time was the Great Obelisk of Axum, and next to it the King Ezana's Obelisk. The Great Obelisk stands ten feet taller at seventy-nine feet, both detailed with intricate carvings. The obelisks mark the graves of Kings and reach so far into the sky that they appear more as a guiding point than a tombstone. There was another obelisk fallen and perfectly cracked into three pieces. The little cemetery had a strange feeling, because of its randomness, and for the sheer size of the obelisks that dwarfed every structure in all of Axum.

At Dire Dawa airport, I tried to get one of the taxis to take me to Harar, but none of them would go beyond the city limits, and they said I must go to the shared-taxi station. On the short Tuk-Tuk ride to the station I witnessed the city's few colonial buildings and generally unremarkable character. Dire Dawa was uneventful and seemed like a less populated version of Addis Ababa. Along the way I saw a dead man at a random spot beside the road. His face bloodied and stock-still. The stillness of death is much different than the stillness of a person at rest. Dead bodies look like all dead things. It was a strange feeling to see a dead man in such a place and drive passed him so quickly. It was a weirdly short experience with death. There was almost no chance to contemplate his life, because no one else was. I continued to think about the man until I was met by the confusion of the shared-taxi station. I was put into a van with fifteen other people. While waiting for the van to fill up there were a few teenage boys who lingered or walked by with clear grocery-sized bags filled with thick green leaves, which they almost constantly stuffed into one side of their mouth. I noticed the bags first and then looked up at their faces, which all carried a glazed look from being incredibly intoxicated from the effects of the Khat. This open use of a kind of drug made me realize I was in a much different part of Ethiopia, and was headed to one that would be even more different. The people were different. There was an intensity about them. The place had the aura of the Wild West, where no one had a chance to enjoy peace or luxury or free time. Life came at them hard. Khat seemed like one way to slow life down and attempt to take control of it. The only people that were sitting were in taxis. No one stopped moving, people even spoke to each other more or less on the move. The one other westerner or white person in sight was put next to me. He was from Sweden. We talked about what we were doing in Ethiopia, refugees in Sweden, and guns in America. I saw him once more in Harar, but after a couple days I lost touch with him like one loses touch with a person at a good party. There was much more to see and do than talk about Stockholm and snow, and American politicians.

I found a guesthouse within the walls of the city. Nearly everyone was pestering me to hold my bag, sell me something or guide me somewhere as I walked through the city. The streets narrowed the closer I got to the gated entrance, which at this point was no longer a street, but an alley that led to another alley and a series of other confusing pedestrian paths. I got a room for ten dollars a night. When the woman running the place told me the price she waited for me to negotiate and was surprised when I quickly agreed to it. There were a couple other westerners staying there, including an older French couple with whom I got a chance to practice French for a couple hours one lazy afternoon. Afterward we went for a walk in the small alleyways and some men would call them out for being French, apparently able to identify them as such, and when they did not buy what one was selling, he loudly proclaimed that all French people are racist. I failed to contain my laughter from the absurdity of the moment, and it seemed as though I was not included in this proclamation. I indeed do not look stereotypically French.

Selling is what Hararis do. There is not much else to do after one has done their prayers. Everyone offers something on the street. They sold aggressively to anyone passing by. It quickly becomes an exhausting occurrence that one has to find their own way of dealing with. Whenever I asked how to get somewhere or do something it was met with an offer to be guided there for a price. Though it was tiring, it became useful at times, because that first night a girl named Aicha who worked around the guesthouse offered to take me to see the Hyena feeding. We met outside the gates around eight at night when it was completely dark. I did not realize just how murky the alleyways were without the presence of any lights. I felt like a fool walking in such a place at night and could not help, but conclude that I was asking for something bad to happen to me. Even with Aicha showing me the way to the main road it did not ease my suspicions of those alleyways. We got in a Tuk-Tuk and drove through the southern gate of the city and then a couple miles down the road to a desolate space that was dimly lit by the presence of several other Tuk-Tuks that had brought the rest of the westerners in Harar to see the Hyenas. The lights all shined at a man sitting on a small rock with a large palm-weaved basket beside him and about twenty Hyenas pacing around. The man grabbed pieces of bloody camel meat from the basket and stuck them on the end of a small stick that a Hyena would quickly lunge at with its thick teeth before scurrying away into the dark. The man would do this several times within a minute and occasionally put the stick in his mouth and a Hyena would then grab the meat. It was certainly a show, but this was no theme park or zoo. It was some dark empty lot on the edge of Harar and amidst a desert. It was just as close to Somalia as it was to Addis Ababa. I took all of this into account when Aicha told me I should sit next to the man to feed some of the Hyenas. I felt no anxiety, and did not worry about anything as I sat down on a rock beside him. The blaring lights of the Tuk-Tuks were discombobulating and the effect was only reduced when a person or Hyena briefly stepped in front of them. The man put his bloody hand on mine and with the other he gave me a stick full of camel meat. Before I could lift it up, the light was dimmed and I was staring at the silhouette of a Hyena about three feet from my face. I could hear the rough breathing, see the wet eyes and the heinous mouth hung open before me. I thought I was going to find out what that mouth felt like on my face or my hand. I was not scared, but I did not want to feel that ugly mouth on me. I raised the stick up and forward, and both the meat and the Hyena were soon gone from my sight. The light then continued to strain my eyes and I continued to watch the man beside me feed the Hyenas from the stick held between his teeth. He got more camel blood on my hands every time he had me feed them.

I stood with Aicha and watched some others do the same, worrying they might get bit by accident. We lingered as most everyone left, to watch the well-fed Hyenas move a bit slower, but now more loudly belted out their notorious laughter. It was somewhat fascinating, but ultimately an unpleasant noise. It was strange to hear it in person and at night, after feeding them. It was a hideous sound and they looked an insecure beast.

We were back in the center of Harar at a cafe overlooking one of the main roundabouts of the city where we sat drinking tea and discussing what we had just seen. It was a calm conversation, but as the minutes went by I began to feel a rush of adrenaline pulsating through me. My heart started to beat quickly, I felt the urge to start running or do some sort of physical activity. The reality of what just happened in that deserted lot suddenly caught up with me. All of my anxiety and adrenaline had somehow been repressed in the moment and now came forth all at once. The high of the experience was on a delay. It was only when the danger and absurdity of the situation was gone that I fully grasped what I had just experienced. I was high and Aicha was not. She had seen this scene over and again her entire life and it was normal to her young and innocent mind.

Hararis have a spiritual connection with the

Hyenas. I do not entirely know the details of this relationship, but there is an affection for them that appears superstitious in nature. Perhaps, similar to Pennsylvanians and their beloved groundhogs. Since there is never a chance of snow in Harar, I presume it is more about good fortune and respect.

Some try to make the Hyena their own. It is easy to love such a hideous and defiant creature that often comes across as an underdog. But the Hyena is a beast of deception. The Hyena's character is more like a vulture or vagrant than a stray dog. They live in packs and rarely prey on an animal by themselves. There is no nobility in the Hyena. We can love it from afar, because it is hungry and hideous, but one should never trust a beastly character for too long. In the vicinity of Harar they are more docile than in the savannah, because they live much of their lives being fed by Hararis. I never grew entirely trustworthy of this beast. This hideous dog. You would like to think the Hyena is an underdog, but it is strong and lowly. The Hyenas I saw were a moderate size as far as Hyenas go. Some can reach much larger and menacing sizes. The larger they are, the more grotesque and dangerous they become.

I was awakened the next morning by the extremely loud call to prayer just before five in the morning. There were no tall buildings around to block the sound of the muezzin and the walls of the old guesthouse were too thin to provide any relief. Once the man's voice hit the first note, the entire city was awakened. God was present and Islam was law. I had heard many a muezzin call before, but there was none so invasive as the one in Harar. It made me realize just how small and isolated a place I was in.

The streets of Harar were busy and overwhelming at times. The people are the pillars of the city. Without them, without the voice of the muezzin there is no Harar. There are no large structures, not even the mosques, to tower over you, shaping the character of the city even when it is covered in darkness. The walls of Harar are the only thing giving form to the city.

I wandered curiously through the streets and found some charming scenes in several places, while buying samosas, bread and coffee from various people on the street. The walls of the houses along alleyways matched the style of the outer walls of the city. There were some splashes of green and blue, but most were painted white. Every wall was layered with dust and dirt, often resembling those without paint.

Never was there an entirely smooth wall or level edge, making the style playful, like Picasso had designed a city. There were similar details in this style dotted around the city. I noticed some at the meat market, but I was quickly distracted by its other characteristics. The edges of the roof were almost entirely lined with vultures who took turns swooping downwards to snatch discarded pieces of meat. It was now midday and the brightness of the sun was contributing to the rank smell of the meat that hung from hooks in each stall. Pieces small and large dangled menacingly from hooks tied to the ceiling and a blood red color was constantly visible. There were discarded pieces of meat and bone in piles outside and beneath the covered walkways. A man sat on the ground hacking away at a portion of some unidentifiable animal with a large cleaver. A cow's head, half-stripped of its skin and meat lie abandoned nearby. The vultures were just as annoying and present as the flies that spun around drunkenly and spoiled for choice. For an outsider it was an impoverished, dirty and somewhat apocalyptic scene, but this was where the people of Harar came to buy meat. Mothers came with their children and the elderly came with small carts to carry their groceries. I had no qualms with it for that reason alone. It was amusing to watch these scenes and imagine the reactions of the more squeamish people I know. I was able to step back and see all perspectives of such a place. I learned to accept some things as they are, for there is little sense in judging such a place. It is a circumstance, but most importantly it is a scene of humanity taking place in the one life that these Hararis had. The people selling meat were not aggressive like others out on the streets selling much different sorts of products. All sales were matter of fact, customers were regular and all interactions were congenial. Prices were set, no haggling was necessary. I enjoyed the scene and decided to sit for some time at one of the small restaurants inside the market to slowly chew on some rice and camel meat. I had eaten camel before in Mongolia and it tasted just as good in Harar.

I woke up the next morning again from the invasive and persistent call to prayer. It was difficult to fall back asleep after waking up in such a startling manor. This did not seem to be the case for anyone else at the guesthouse for there was no one up making or sipping coffee in the courtyard. The sky barely had any light in it when I opened the front gate and was met with the scene of a dog chewing on the cheek of a cow's head. The body was nowhere in sight. This little alleyway was about a meter wide and I had to gingerly step around the dog and his breakfast. The dog gave me an indifferent look and was much more focused on the task at hand. There was surprisingly no blood on the ground and I could only assume that it had been drained out sometime before it found its way to my doorstep. The only other detail was a small rope tied around the head that stretched out on the ground. I tried over and again to imagine the moment it landed in this spot, but I was continually interrupted by the sound of the little dog chewing away on its face. If the muezzin had not woken me up then this scene certainly made it so I would not be going back to sleep anytime soon. Either way, I had the urge for some more of the local coffee, which I was quickly becoming addicted to. Coffee was never far and I bought some from a lady who gave away free coffee and bread to each person unable to buy any. Her stall was a makeshift setup along a congested street.

I found myself near one of the city's gates where there was a maze of busy streets. When I turned the corner of one I was met by a crowd of people standing around a large camel that lie dead on the dusty street. The people seemed to all be talking at the same time as three men with large knives contemplated and positioned themselves around the unmoving beast. An argument broke out among the men and the crowd as everyone grew anxious and inched closer. A couple of men controlled the crowd and one began cutting into the stomach of the camel. It was a long continuous cut that took the shape of a rectangle with one side left uncut. The large flap of flesh was flung open like a door and revealed a massive pile of stomach and intestines. All of the innards wobbled as the skin was folded over to the side. The crowd cried out in delight. When the two other men joined in with the first, blood began to pour out onto the ground creating a pool of red around the camel. The stomach was recklessly cut open, which led to all the shit and bile pouring out onto the ground and mixing with the blood. The dirty green color turned everything on the ground into mud and the wretched smell was inescapable even from twenty feet away. All the kids in the crowd grew more excited while the adults kept positioning themselves close to the men doing the cutting. A little girl standing next to me was the only one I saw pinching her nose shut. The men started to hand out pieces of meat to women in the crowd, dropping them in small plastic bags or directly into their hands. A few teenage boys stood on the edge of the crowd laughing at the whole scene while a middle aged man proclaimed that an entire leg belonged to him as soon as it was cut off at the hip. He tied a rope around the ankle and struggled to drag the large leg up the street. I followed him as he descended down a hill picking up speed and every young child nearby ran along with him cheering. Back at the carcass it was a bloody mess that looked like a homicide had taken place as the camel had now become unrecognizable. A man dragging half-a-rack of ribs with a rope in the same direction the other man went. One leg remained, as did the head and some other random parts. The smell was horrendous as every liquid once inside the camel was now spread out in a circle twenty feet in diameter. As I watched the men continue to cut what was left of the camel, a young woman came up to me and started asking me questions. She was not interested in what I thought of the scene before us, but where I was staying, how old I was and if I was alone. I answered her questions and she pointed down a street beyond the camel and told me she lived just down there before giving me her number.

The smells and savagery of the camel's carcass coupled with the crowd's desperation to get a piece of meat was intense. When it all subsided I pulled myself away and wandered the streets for a couple of hours pondering the surreality of the scene. I was in two minds about it. I was excited by its madness and savagery, but saddened by the poverty of it all. I reminded myself that most of the people there had carried smiles on their faces and did not appear unsure about much. I found a place to eat and sip some tea before wandering over to the meat market in the mid-afternoon on my way back to my room. I spoke to some of the butchers I saw the day before, asking them how their day had been going. When I mentioned that I had seen a camel get slaughtered in the street they looked at me with shocked expressions. "You saw that?!" One man exclaimed. "Those men, they were arrested."

Apparently it was illegal to do such a thing. More specifically it was haram(forbidden) because it was not Halal. Muslims were not allowed to eat meat from an animal that had merely died. That kind of meat was to be left for other animals and nature's course. It was necessary to kill and bless it at the same time in accordance with Islamic law. The news of the imprisonment added to the mayhem of thoughts now swirling in my mind. I resigned myself back to the courtyard of the guesthouse and helped one of the workers paint one of the interior walls a beautiful mint green.

There was nothing grand about the courtyard, but when the sun shined down from directly above it was a congenial place to sit and drink copious cups of coffee and speak to whoever walked through the gates. It had the feel of a home and the social atmosphere of a cafe. Aicha was there most days and a stream of European travelers would come through for a night or two. There was also a man named Moti who was always around and worked as a guide like most other people. He was funny and always talking to me about girls he could get for me or what he did with some girl the night before.

I had no need for a guide until he took me and a British couple named Ollie and Leila, who had been traveling around Africa for six months, out to the Babille camel market. It was a two-hour drive east into the desert towards Somalia. The landscape became dry and more rugged as we went. The small villages were quiet except when there were some teenagers along the road who would threaten to throw a rock at the car.

In order to get to Babille we had to cross into another region known as Oromo. We came to the checkpoint and we were pulled aside by a police officer. He and Moti calmly argued for a little while and eventually Moti returned to the car defeated. The cop stood there looking about indifferently. He was expressionless, sometimes talking to others and simply waiting for a bribe. After another twenty minutes I grew bored and impatient and bluntly asked him what the problem was and why he was holding us up. This somewhat startled him and the expression on his face changed. I do not know why, but he tapped the hood of the car and waved us through.

The town of Babille was impoverished and rural.

The red earth all around consumed my eyes. The streets were crowded with people, and herds of goats and sheep being led down to the market. It felt like being in an ancient or even biblical setting and everything modern seemed out of place, including the cars. The camel market consisted of a large concrete wall in the shape of a jagged rectangle on an even piece of land. The shepherds were rough with the camel. Without hesitation they used large sticks to slap the camels on the neck or the backside in order to move them along or behave as they wished. The shepherds were mostly young men that carried a casual confidence and expressions that were decidedly content. They were cracking jokes with most who came by and when we asked how much the camels were one replied that he was interested in buying Leila.

No one bought Leila nor did any of us buy a camel or any other livestock. Just a few coffees before getting back on the road. There was no bribe or conversation necessary to leave Oromo province, but an hour into the ride back to Harar a few dozen young men stood in the middle of the road blocking our path. I sat in the front and when we came to a complete stop the men had their hands in the car and were shouting faranjo at us. I was used to being called faranjo at this point as I had been called it so many times in every part of Ethiopia I had visited. Without looking at the driver I said, "you might want step on the gas," which he did and parted the sea of men before us. A few of the same young boys along the road again threatened to throw rocks at the car. It was a rough landscape, seemingly rife with banditry for there were many places to hide or shoot from. I was relieved to be back in the courtyard before sundown.

A couple days later I met up with Moti at the meat market to buy some camel meat for a lunch he was to prepare. We walked through the streets to a house and Moti had some brief and congenial words with a young woman in the street. "She wants me to eat her," he said to me with a smile. A few hundred meters further along another girl spoke to Moti, and he said to me with a smile, "I already ate her. You can have her if you like." Wherever we stopped, the girls were pretty. I pointed one out to him and he said, "she can be your wife very easily."

I sat on the rug in a courtyard of a house being served cup after cup of delicious coffee that was cooked, ground and poured in front of me by a nice elderly lady. Moti was at work making a large camel curry. Some other people joined us and soon we were all laid out on the rug and pillows in a food coma. The siesta was not over when Moti asked me if I wanted to chew some Khat. I gave him some money and he disappeared for about half-an-hour before returning with a large clear bag full of green leaves. We made our way to a Khat den that consisted of a room with four levels of wide steps. Each level already had one or two men lounging on a carpet chewing almost constantly, picking from a pile of leaves in front of them and putting them into the side of their mouth. I found a spot at the top level beside a Turkish man named Mohammed. I took my time chewing a leaf or two, because I was still in a sleepy state from the large meal we had just eaten. Mohammed told me to take a pinch of sugar with each bite until I got used to the bitter taste of the Khat. An hour went by and I was still sleepy, but I continued to converse with Mohammed. I told him to explain to me all the steps one had to partake during Hajj. I knew what they were, but I always enjoyed listening to Muslims speak about this endeavor. It is the pinnacle of their life as a believer and never are they not happy to explain this. For nearly two hours I listened to Mohammed talk while we chewed Khat with sugar and were served round after round of fresh coffees cooked right in front of us. Moti chewed Khat on the lower level and left several times to do God only knows what. Another hour went by and it was now me who was doing all the talking to Mohammed and then a few of the other men who joined in on the conversation about politics, America, women and anything else we felt like. After four hours of chewing Khat I was wide awake and on a roll getting everyone to laugh as much as possible. Ollie and Leila showed up toward the end and we left together with Moti. It was now dark and walking through the unlit alleyways was sobering. We made our way to a bar just outside the walls of the city. We sat on the sidewalk drinking beer with Muslims that was brewed by Muslims, hoping that some Hyenas would come to the nearby dumpsters for some food. Leila said their journey was at an end and they should fly home soon. "I'm tired of all the racism. I'm tired of being the white-girl in Africa," she proclaimed. Moti was becoming more drunk and insisted on us going to a nightclub. We followed him into the dark streets to a small club that had few people inside. It felt like nothing good could come of such a place. The music played at an absurdly loud volume, and I could not hear anything anyone said. We sat just outside so that we could hear each other and Moti began ranting like drunk people do. He kept saying, "I don't know why anyone is racist, I don't know why anyone discriminates, I love all people, black people, white people, everyone is my brother, everyone is my friend, I don't understand hatred." The more he went on like this the less I believed him, he started to just sound like a drunk person who was making himself feel good by saying dreamy things in order to gain friends and affection.

I agreed with him hoping that it would make him talk about something else, but every time I agreed he went on and on about it saying how much he loved everyone on earth. I tried to put him at rest again by saying I knew how he felt, and that I had a gay cousin who had a black boyfriend. Before I could even finish that sentence, the look on his face turned to one of disgust and a long disapproving grunt bellowed from his mouth. Ollie looked at me and said, "you opened up a can of worms, mate." Moti looked at me differently, it was akin to offending him personally. He quickly said, "that's disgusting, why would he do that? We kill those people!" Eventually, I was able to change the subject and distract his mind with more drinks. We soon left, and Moti was now very drunk and loud as we walked through the murky streets. Moti was the only person or thing that could be heard. It felt as though the police were going to arrest us for making all this noise in such a quiet place. Ollie and Leila broke away and walked down the main street of Harar to where they were staying and Moti insisted on guiding me through the alleyways to the guesthouse. When we got to the gate he asked for some money for the Khat and beers even though I had already paid for both. I gave him some more and he asked what time we should meet the next day. I told him in the afternoon knowing that I would be leaving early in the morning. He smiled and disappeared into the dark alleyway and I could hear his shouting and singing become less forceful the further away he went.

I managed to sleep for about two hours and then walked out of the gate of the guesthouse as the call to prayer rung out. I felt protected by the noise while I walked through the murky streets thinking anyone intent on having a go at me would be momentarily distracted by it. I was just outside the walls of the city when I looked back at the main gate that framed a golden sunrise behind the city. It was an image I will never let myself forget for it made me wonder what I might encounter in the streets had I stayed.

The shared taxi was soon over the mountains and descending towards Dire Dawa. When we reached the city limits I felt like I was in another country and the feeling of Harar was as far away as any place on earth. I missed it. I thought how that little city was a jewel and a great secret, because it was enveloped in the spirit of rebellion, it was wild, and it was free.

I ordered two coffees from the bar at Tomoca. I sat talking and drinking coffee for a couple hours and admired the quotes of Balzac on signs hanging from the ceiling. "When you drink a cup of coffee, ideas come marching in like an army." I was not as displeased with Addis Ababa as I had been on my previous arrival. It was hot outside and the atmosphere of the cafe felt like a retreat. I was full of caffeine, and decided to walk the three miles back to my hotel. The sun beat down on me and I broke a sweat. I marched forward, not always knowing if I was headed in the right direction. I made it to the hotel, and the next day I made it to the airport. And it was only when the plane took off that I realized, not once had I thought about Arthur Rimbaud.

October 16th, 2022
Paris